A POSITIVE CONCEPT

TO END DOMESTIC VIOLENCE

AUTHOR
DESIREE L WOODS

ILLUSTRATIONS
ROSHANAY FATIMA

1

GEM
A Positive Commute
To End Domestic Violence©
Copyright 2024

For information address:
Desiree L Wooods
DayMart Textile Services & Outlet, LLC
2785 E Grand Boulevard Detroit, MI 48202
daymart.services@gmail.com

While He's Messing Up Your Mind

Wake up dear, and adhere

Love ain't blind,

So free your mind.

This is not but a steppingstone

On the road to higher heights

And deeper depths.

Don't lose the fight,

Keep high your sight

And don't stop until you reach the top.

One day you will find

your love and kind

Come right to you.

Don't be set back

Stay on the right track.

Victory begins in a dream

Accomplished in what is done

Glory to the Son, cause in my life I won-

No matter What!

ABOUT THE AUTHOR

Desiree L. Woods is a Christian writer, Detroit-native with southern roots, entrepreneur, and mentor. She is inspired to write books to help people struggling with issues as further described. She uses her ability to capture the core of the problems and provide comfort, hope and resources. She is the author behind this book Part two of a Trilogy: 'Gem – A Positive Commute – To End Domestic Violence: and 'Part One -Tina–Unexpected Pleasures, Unanticipated Pain – sub tittle 'Abstractions & Hindsight': Addressed to Teen Moms & their Families: Part Three 'Wormhole Imbroglio to Disengage' Freedom from Substance Abuse. She is also the author of 'You Can Say That-The Doors We Close', To help you recognize the signs of inappropriate behaviors and to comfort those struggling with sexual trauma in hope of getting past the distresses. She speaks that she knows and is a testament of what she has seen.

She has experienced sexual trauma, been a Teen Mom; Escaped Domestic Violence and had a bout with Substance Abuse, and now is victorious over all those areas, and desires to help others to transition triumphantly.

INTRODUCTION

Domestic violence is not just toward women. Statistics states that about 1 in 3 men experienced sexual violence, physical violence, or have been stalked by an intimate partner during their lifetime.

In this book are delicate situations about two incidents a woman and a man. There are also references of nameless individuals. In most cases the names and relationships have been changed to protect the innocent.

If you are in a domestic violence situation, please I beg you to make a plan to get out! Today there is help and multiple routes to escape. In this book you will also see the dangers that can occur if you stay, in which the outcomes can lead ultimately to death even murder-suicide.

If fearful, that's okay, make your move anyway from the danger zone fearful! The fear will dissipate. The anxiety you feel will lift the closer you get to safety. In all cases you must move with wisdom, its important that you **<u>don't look back</u>**!

OBJECTIVE OF THIS BOOK

The objective of this book is to give you support and encourage you to devise a plan to get up and get out. To give you hope for a bright future no matter what your position in life or neighborhood you live in.

The two scenarios listed are very drastic but true. The names and relationships have been altered to protect the innocent.

I want you to notice the 'red flags' and 'triggers' so you can recognize them in your own life. I hope you see clearly the danger and consequences if you stay: and the illumination of hope, satisfaction and victory when you go!

There is much more support now and social emergence then it was when it happened to me. The way is made easier to make the shift confidentially with or without children. If you must leave with nothing, try to have your ID, driver's license birth certificate(s) or passports, Social Security Card with you, if it's too dangerous to attain, safety first.

Synopsis of Resources

I'm placing this information in front just in case you don't have time to read the whole book or jump to the back.

National Domestic Violence Hotline
800-799-SAFE (800-799-7233)
SMS: Text START to 99788
www.thehotline.org

When using the Domestic Violence website, if you have to get off quickly without a trace-double click on the red 'X' in upper right-hand corner. It automatically erases the history.

National Domestic Violence Hotline
800-799-SAFE (800-799-7233)
Text: START to 99788
www.thehotline.org

Strong Hearts Native Help line
1-844-7NATIVE (762-8483)
www.strongheartshelpline.org

DoD Safe Helpline (Department of Defense)
877-995-5247

Nationally wherever you are, you can google:

>Domestic Violence Shelter

>Domestic Violence hotline

>Nonprofit Domestic Violence Counselor

There are more in the back of the book

!Warning!

If you are reading this book and in a domestic violence situation, please don't have the book on your person where the perpetrator can get hold of it. Leave it with a friend, relative or place that the perpetrator does not have access to.

The reason why these series are short is because getting to the point is pertinent, so that you can be free.

.

The hotline is listed throughout the book, as well as listings for Safe Houses, Counseling and Resources in case your reading is made short.

There are no addresses listed except offices or telephone numbers for security purposes. The phone call, Text or Chat will get you to the person that will assist in getting you to the right and secure place.

About the Cover

The name was chosen because a Gem is a precious stone, especially when cut, polished or engraved. I think of you as a Priceless Gem. You may need polishing; the dust of manipulation, low self-esteem and abuse dusted off you and wrong doers cut from your life: positive declarations, aspirations and motivations engraved in you.

As a stone, that hurt shame and abuse don't have to breach you any longer. When you go through the process, you will gleam as a Precious Jewel in your rightful place.

Herein is a blueprint of a plan, supportive people, services and your way up and out. Let's walk-through your new season.

To you I foretell that you will come out, and you will go forth and have success beyond the bleakness.

This book will enlighten, encourage and guide you to a new destiny that looks better than you look right now.

LET'S DISCUSS RED FLAGS

Red flags are warning signs that indicate unhealthy or manipulative behavior, that is not always recognized at first, that's what makes it so dangerous, they become bigger and more problematic over time.

Below are some examples of red flags in relationships:

- ✓ Rude behavior or aggression
- ✓ Controlling, manipulation
- ✓ Don't have friends or run away your friends i.e.
- ✓ Don't show support to you or other relationships.
- ✓ Sarcasm and criticism
- ✓ Deceit
- ✓ Jealousy
- ✓ Lack of, or unhealthy communication
- ✓ Living in the past
- ✓ Toxic behaviors -Addictions
- ✓ Unforgiveness
- ✓ Not willing to compromise
- ✓ Lack of trust
- ✓ Being on the edge or feeling uneasy
- ✓ lying or hiding the truth

GEM - A POSITIVE COMMUTE TO END DOMESTIC VIOLENCE

HER STORY

TABLE OF CONTENT

HER STORY

First, I must paint you a picture of where she was before the altercation. Everything was beautiful up until that point. I want you to see the first red flags that went up, that was totally ignored. know that it would have changed the trajectory of the whole outcome.

It was a warm day for a walk. Breeze was blowing softly in her face and the sun was shining. It was a perfect day for a walk downtown. She was thinking happy thoughts, then suddenly She was approached by a gentleman that started walking beside her and keeping up with her pace. He was suave, a smooth talker, he looked nice, clean cut, well-groomed and smelling good. To make a long story short, they ended up at a restaurant eating brunch and shooting the breeze.

HER STORY

Let's go back. Her name on the set was well known, had a business called 'Head to Toe' and Hair Broidery. The motto she chose for designing cloths was: "I'll look you over and measure you up, jot down your style and work it out, for you…The Unique Personality", her motto for Hair Broidery was: Braids & Weaves add volume, color length. It was a one stop shop for men, women and couples.

She also modeled hair for the local hair Stylist and Hair-Hat Designer, Delores Wisdom, who won awards in United States and Europe for her Hair Hat designs. All was wonderful!

She also met a doctor finishing school, that was complaining about how heavy the medical books were and had an idea to do Totes on Wheels. I said, "Great idea, I'll get back with a prototype." (This was long before they were popular.

HER STORY

She was working on some orders for custom Salon Jackets; acquired another industrial sewing machine with anticipation of doing the Totes; and sketched the prototype for the Tote-on-Wheels. Opportunity was looking great!

Now to get back to where I left off. So, she made it a point to ask the gentleman, "This brunch is without strings attached, right?" and he replied, "Right, no strings attached". So, they ate as they continued to talk. The felt as if they had known each other for years.

Afterwards he asked her what she was going to do and she replied, "shop for shoes". He accompanied her. She eyed some shoes that were desirable. He offered to pay for them, she said, "No", but after she tried them on, he kept insisting. She said again, "No strings attached?" and he replied, "No strings attached". You're sure? He confirmed.

HER STORY

So, moving forward they had a lot of late-night conversations. She never asked him where he worked, where the money was coming from or why She don't see him at night. Later on, you will find out the answers to those questions.

Time moved on. It appeared that he worked and had an income. He was also very nice to her children, especially around Christmas. Time went on and feeling comfortable with him, she let him move in with her and her children. Now let's go back to the Doctor. He ended up with a jealous girlfriend, so that cut off their business relationship. So, she continued with the idea herself. Guess what? She ended up with someone jealous too and didn't want Her to work! He said he'll take care of her and her children. In time the situation turned. She couldn't do hair or sew. She couldn't hang out with her, if friends it wasn't concerning her immediate household. girls. Her outings were with him and his family and to speed up the story:

HER STORY

Now let's go back to the Doctor. He ended up with a jealous girlfriend, so that cut off their business relationship. So, she said, she can do it on her own. Guess what? She ended up with someone that didn't want Her to work! He said he'll take care of her and her children.

In time the situation turned. She couldn't do hair or sew. She couldn't hang out with her girls. Her outings were with him and his family and friends, if it wasn't concerning her immediate household.

To speed up the story. She eventually realized her phonebook was now filled with his relatives and friends. When her girlfriends would come over, he would run them away! When people would call her for business, he would tell them, she was unavailable. This is before everyone had mobile phones if you can imagine that. Mobile phones were out, but the diplomats had them and they were attached to cars. Pagers were popular then.

HER STORY

One time she was over his mother's house and she said, "Don't make him mad". She asked her what did she mean by that? She said, "Just don't make him mad". Of course that was a challenge for her. I wanted to know what would happen if he got angry, was he going to turn into Mr. Hyde!

One of the conversations we had earlier was that he was a recovering alcoholic. She never saw or smelled alcohol on his breathe so to her, he beat it.

One day, the first time ever she saw him full of alcohol and babbling. She asked him what set him off. He told her what it was and she cannot tell us in this setting. They talked about counseling, and he agreed to go and she supported him. He also started taking Antabuse. I was told that is supposed to neutralize the alcohol in his system and it would make him sick if he were to drink on it.

HER STORY

Let's go back now. When she asked him about his wife earlier when they first met, before they lived together, he said she was dead. The moment he said that she heard a voice say so clearly, "He killed her". She did not ask him the circumstances of her death. She smoothed it over and went to the next subject.

She later asked his brother the circumstances of his wife's death and he told her he killed her. I guess she made him made! To explain why she never saw him at night in the beginning, he was in a halfway house and had just come out of prison from killing his wife. He only did six months for that crime, since his mother-in-law testified on his behalf, that he was a good husband, father and provider to his family and it was an accident. How crazy is that! She remembered coming in one night, he had been drinking and the next thing she knew, the back of her neck was on the bar of the clothing rack, and he had her vocal cords in a grip as to separate it from her body!

HER STORY

She couldn't scream, breath or fight. I just staired at him. After a while he said, "You must want me to kill you!" then he let her go.

He became very apologetic afterward. He told her how sorry he was. Being romantic and holding her close to him. Had great sex, she let him but, in her mind, she wasn't taking it anymore! The next day he came home with gifts and money saying he'll never do it again.

She let some weeks go pass. Then when he was in a good mood and not drinking, she told him that we had rushed into the relationship, we should give each other a little space; sometime to think things over. We're not breaking up just giving each other a little space. He moved out.

HER STORY

She got back into doing hair and sewing but he was constantly calling her, asking if he could take her to the grocery store or to dinner: she declined of course.

When I had customers over or was sewing, his presence was out in the parking lot as if he was fixing his car or talking to a neighbor.

When she had customers for hair or was sewing, she had big picture windows in living room and would leave the blinds open wide to take advantage of the sun and would notice him present in the parking lot, looking under the hood of his car or talking to a neighbor. This made her quite suspicious of him.

Let me go back. From the day of meeting him, every night she had the same reoccurring nightmare; her running from roof to roof, hearing a loud bang, then fall off the roof: but would wake up before she hit the ground. Every single night this would happen! This went on for almost a year.

HER STORY

She finally told my girlfriend about it, she lived in Cleveland. They both agreed, it was time to get out of dodge! Girlfriend said, "Ain't nothing to it, but to do it!". So, she packed her kid's bags, her bags, and her girlfriend came, packed the Audi and they headed to Cleveland, Ohio.

Let me take you back. Before she left, she put a 'tap' on the phone" so the police could trace the calls. Back then you had to fill out forms to have your phone 'Tapped' via Michigan Bell, and she connected the phone to an answering machine.

When she left for Cleveland, she put newspaper up to the window to give the house the appearance that she had moved out.

While I was there in Cleveland, she found out that it was not easy to be an upcoming black female entrepreneur doing it the same way It was done in Detroit. Some of the obstacles was that the local newspaper would not create a column for her craft, Hair. In Cleveland she could get $350 a head for the styles she was doing for $100 & $150. dollars in Detroit. So, only through word of mouth or circulating flyers on postcard stock was she able to get the word out.

That meant she had to have money up front and do a lot of leg work. she was still paying for a townhouse and utilities in Detroit. On top of that she had 5 children and 3 of them were in band and came with her. The summer is ending it's time to go back to school, she had to make a decision. Was she going to give up the townhouse and start all over or go back.

As she was contemplating her girlfriend told her to call her house. In her mind that sounded stupid, for one thing the machine was on silent and nobody was supposed to be there, but she did it anyway. Lo and behold guess who answers the phone? He did! He answered the phone and she hung up! She was enraged! She decided in that moment that the devil wasn't going to make her run. The Lord said the devil will flee! She packed her kids up and went back to her townhouse.

Everything seemed to be ok for a while. She repaired the window he came through in the basement with plexiglass. She got a gun. At first, She had a 357. Magnum but by her never shooting a gun and was told it takes someone that is familiar with that type of gun to be accurate, she gave it back to the owner.

She was on her way to get a shotgun and a friend took her to the pawn shop unknowingly that she was going to purchase a shotgun. Once he found out he said he had a 22. Caliber she could use.

Moving forward. It's now April Fool's Day, April 1, 1986. He puts some flowers and house shoes at her door. The next day she's at the house, kept her 5-year-old and 7-year-old out of school that day, they had a half day, so she could braid their hair. She's upstairs.

HER STORY

Suddenly she hears a noise. She knows he's in the house. She told the girls to go into the other room and close the door. She quickly ran and got her pistol. She runs to the top of the steps and he's at the bottom. She warned him if he comes any closer, she will shoot him. He came running and she pulled the trigger. She heard a little pop like a fire cracker and no sign that she had hit him. He came charging after her like a bull! She ran in her room, closed and locked the door. Now the door had a deadbolt lock on it, he kicked the door in and she tried shooting the gun again and it jammed!

They wrestled with that gun seem like for an hour. He finally got it from her, had her pinned to the floor face down, with the gun put to the back of her head execution style. She said if you shoot me, you'll kill me. He said, "l don't care" and pulled the trigger! To her surprise she was still alive, as fluid filled her ears she laid there as if she was dead. She heard him tell the girls to go into the closet. I knew then he was going to set the house on fire!

HER STORY

She got up and ran to the widow, her neighbor was on the porch. She yelled at her to call the police, she had been shot. He came running in the room as she climbed out the window and was hanging from the ledge. He came and tried to shoot the gun but it jammed again. He began to hit her hands with the butt of the gun until she fell from the second floor.

She remembered by then the police and ambulance had come as well as her oldest son and brother. She found out later when her girlfriend brought her the Detroit Free Press. (She was on the second front page)
She was so afraid. The detectives put a guard at her room as they explained to her that he drove himself to the hospital, she had just missed his heart, and the gun she had was a piece of $%#&! I still feel today that he shot himself. The way he came after me like a bull and wrestled with me he could not have been shot; I know it had to be self-inflicted! Suicide-murder gone wrong! Thank you, Jesus!

HER STORY

I just want to say that I was blessed! The Doctors couldn't do anything because surgery would paralyze my left side or be fatal. They were amazed that I was still living! The bullet fragments are a permanent fixture to my skull. They made sure I was safe during my hospital stay. I am a walking Miracle!

I had a few domestic violence relationships before this, but they were not quite as bad and I got out of them quickly!

Hindsight: When the unction came to me that he had killed his wife, I should have not continued to get close to him. I should have said, "Nice meeting you, Good bye" and made my exit! He would not have ever known why! I could have avoided getting my vocal cords almost pulled out, losing my friends, and my business relations. I would not have had to move to Ohio. By the Grace of God, He saved me out of a bad situation. I'm Alive! Maybe it's just to warn you, to recognize the red flags in the early stage, the first meeting stage, don't let it get to the dating stage:

and if you are in a toxic relationship, recognize and make a plan to get out! If you've moved free from the situation don't do like I did and second guess and go back. Don't let the 'triggers' get you caught up. Recognize the triggers the emotions that would make you stay or go back. Mine was pride yes, the Lord said, "The enemy will flee." But the first part of that scripture is 'Submit yourself to God, resist the devil, and he will free from you.' I should have moved forward. I should have let the past go and start all over. I had help I could have gotten a job. I was connected to people that had connections to employment. That was my second, and third chance that the Lord had given me, I had other skills but, even so God made a way of escape out of a bad situation. Wait a minute, I did not go back to him. I went back to my house, what was familiar to me but also known to him.

Even if you think you don't have skills there are other jobs that calls for just knowing how to talk to people, and knowing how to resolve conflict and be nice; and just being dependable; they will train you as a new hire.

HER COMMENTS

Be wise on how you protect yourself in any situation, just go – and get out - and don't look back! Be nice until it is safe to flee. Don't talk about what you should do think about it…make it happen! Oh of course fight back don't be nobody's pouching bag when possible. I had no strength compared to his and of course I was ignorant on how to use a gun and got shot with my own pistol. But in my situation, I was no match for a physical fight. Be wise in getting other people involved to protect you in any situation. How could you live knowing they got hurt because of you, (unless it's the police or someone trained in that matter) helping you. Even that is only temporary. It's far better to get others involved to help by moving forward to a safe place always.

GEM - A POSITIVE COMMUTE
TO END DOMESTIC VIOLENCE

ANTHOLOGY

HINDSIGHT

I Could Have Loved You Forever

Your voice was kind but strong.

We would conversate all day long.

You were gentle with me.

Introduced me to a passion I knew not.

Showed me you cared about family and

I didn't have to ask you for anything.

I fell easily for you but,

when you pushed my friends away,

isolated me from my aspirations & inspirations.

You put your hands on me to hurt me, to even kill me.

How can feelings go from Love to Hate,

Comfort to Harm! You see, it wasn't love in the

beginning it was lust, a sensual appetite!

The result is no love, no peace, no kindness.

What you wanted was to control,

Only wanted what made you feel good.

So, you were all puffed up in yourself,

a gentleman, was your psychotic front.

I Could Have Loved You Forever

Seeking your own desires,

So easily provoked to think evil.

You actually delighted in some secret immoral act.

You couldn't bear to see me happy outside of you.

Why didn't you believe I could love others,

my dreams, my aspirations and love you too.

You couldn't hold on to see that maybe,

these things would enhance our relationship.

Your love failed because it wasn't love.

It was lust from the very beginning to the end.

By Desiree L Woods

UNSURE

You say you love me

I'm unsure, you say you need me

But I am not your cure:

You swore not to cheat

or beat me but, yet

you have executed all

of those things above.

You brought more pain than good,

More anger than joy,

More cheating than purity

More fear than trust

More fuss than hugs:

but you claim to love me.

I know this ...you will never ever be

anything more to me, not even my friend.

By Maria Denise

AN AWAKENING

I started writing a letter of release.

I had the music on and the pen was non-stop.

A song came on, I put my high heels on

I began to dance. I even looked in the mirror

I liked who I saw. I put the pen down and

I washed some cloths. Had a meal with some relatives,

laughed joked, had a good time, then made my way

home.

I was my old self again, the Self that had no

restrictions.

Motivated with a mindset that there is a solution

to every problem.

I am an overcomer; no obstacles can stop me!

By Desire L. Woods

NIGHTTIME

I went to sleep and my dreams were of terror.
I awakened and thought someone was in my bedroom.
I charged toward the image as if to erase its presence.
Then I saw the image as it was, just cloths hanging.
I drank some water and went back to sleep, but not
before I pleaded the Blood of Jesus, I talked to the
Lord until I feel asleep. In my spirit affirming the
things God has said, who He is and what He can do.
I prayed that my sleep would be sweet and so it was.

I went back to sleep and woke up, looked at the time.
Time to Get ready for Church. Suddenly the spirit of
fear fell on me so heavy and I had to immediately pray
it off and declare it would not hold me hostage! And so
it departed!
I am walking in faith under the shadow of the
Almighty! I will not fear what man can do to me and
I know without a shadow of doubt that God is on my
side, He is more than the world against me!
All power is in His hand, He is the Highest Power!

THE MORNING AFTER

As I made my way to church, I was conscience of danger. It was a dust of snow coming down and when I ran my wipers the fluid did not come out, windshield smeared, I couldn't see! Looking down under the smear, I had to immediately come off the freeway.

I pulled over as soon as I could and threw snow on my windshield, ran the wipers a few times and went on my way.

I almost got into three more accidents after that, Praise God for my guardian angels, I made it to the church safe!

The message at church was about demonic attacks and what to do to shield from their antics, their grotesque or bizarre behaviors and influences.

Morning by morning new mercies I find!

DISCUSSIONS ABOUT HER STORY

No matter where you are, there are safe houses and a way of escape. There was not in place in her situation what is available today to escape. The police at that time weren't concerned until it was too late. There were no safe houses or conversations concerning domestic violence. Today there are mobile phones, text to phone, Supportive Services, Safe Houses, Hot Lines, Prayer lines, churches, people, counseling and a host of services and agencies across the country. Some are listed throughout the book and city specific but if your city is not listed:

National Domestic Violence Hotline

800-799-SAFE | 800-799-7233

Text: START to 99788

www.thehotline.org

the national hotline can find support in your city of refuge for you.

MY HARDHEADED SISTER

I said don't do it
Not once, not twice
But many times!
I've said go don't stay
Run for your life!

You seem to enjoy pain
And love to disobey regardless of
The cost you seem to think
You're the boss.

So, what shall I do My
Little hardheaded Sister?
What will it take for you to just
Listen, learn and obey?
Will it take a rape?
Will it take a loss?

MY HARDHEADED SISTER

Will it take more discipline?

Or your life to end?

Yes, this is serious! No more games!

You won't to achieve esteem? But you

will endure more pain for

not listening to what we all say:

Now who is to blame?

What will you have to gain?

My Hardheaded Sister…

by Maria Denise

DISCUSSIONS ABOUT HER STORY

Her Story is unique because she had divine intervention. It is divine so I can alert you. Red flags were seen in the very beginning. Her spirit got the unction that he killed his wife as well as other red flags throughout the relationship. The bad dreams, the isolation, jealousy, controlling, manipulative spirit, and the addiction.

Since then, she heard of women that suffered the same injuries and didn't make it. Women that went back and lost their life. Not that God won't intervene in your situation, but maybe he let her live so that she could warn you of the danger of staying in an abusive relationship.

Remember, she left and went back in the same house, although they had separated, he knew the address. God let death sweep over her so she could warn you, especially if you are reading this book. Recognized your red flags. Have you had the unction to leave? Then Go and don't look back!

DISCUSSIONS ABOUT HER STORY

Please take courage and make a roadmap to escape and have it written in your mind, not on a piece of paper! Prepare…Fear not, but if you're fearful, go scared! There is a way of escape.

www.ncadv.org

National Hotline

(800-799-7233)

Opals Project

Exiting Domestic Violence

737-225-3150

Text: START to **99788**

GEM - A POSITIVE COMMUTE
TO END DOMESTIC VIOLENCE

HIS STORY

HIS STORY

His family moved into a new housing complex, there also was a neighbor with seven brothers and one sister and she got his attention. She didn't give him the time of day at first because she was in a relationship. That relationship became abusive and he became her knight in shining armor; who in time saved her from an abusive relationship. Down the road they got married and quickly he fathered a child.

The marriage was good until years later by means of a relative, who found divorce papers stating he had been married before her; (although it was an arranged marriage, that had never been consummated). He showed the paperwork to his wife. He also told her that he had formally proposed to an older lady, that did not except his proposal: and that he was still friends with the brother and sister of that lady, and the godfather of her sister's daughter.

So, this was the beginning of the distrust. She could never understand those relationships or get past him not

HIS STORY

Unforgiveness And Verbal Abuse

telling her in the beginning that he had been married previously and also had a rejected proposal.

The verbal abuse began. This abuse went on for about 10 years with verbal attacks and lack of trust. Her taking his phone and most times destroying it, and destroying his cloths and belongings.

He divorced her 10 years in. Everybody thought he had gone crazy; (he never told family of the abuse he was going through).

He changed his hair from wearing a ponytail to Finger Waves, got a Red Drop Top Camaro and his own apartment. It appeared that those were the best times of his life, he was a free spirit.

On the other hand, his wife was constantly crying to his Auntie about how she missed him. Like I said, nobody knew about the abuse. She cried about how much she loved him and wanted him back.

HIS STORY

Finally, his Auntie convinced him to go back to her, without knowing the facts of why he left her in the first place.

Well, he went back being deceived by all her sweet talk and false affection. Happiness lasted for about two months. She started constantly throwing in his face the past and restart on the verbal abuse that now extended in front of friends and family and continued when they were alone.

But when the money came, she was sweat as apple pie and when the money was exhausted or got thin near the end of the month and he refused to give her more money; the abuse continued.

Then she started using other manipulative tactics to try to get other people to dislike him by saying that the only daughter he had was not his. The family knew that but accepted her no matter what.

HIS STORY

He couldn't have friends over and when his friends would come to pick him up; when he got home his cloths were destroyed by pouring bleach on them or mustard and ketchup all over them. She would take his phone look through it, keep it or destroy it.

Later, his daughter had a daughter who grew up and had a daughter. The joy of his life! The wife was jealous of any relationship her husband would have outside of her, even the great-granddaughter that he loved so much.

She wouldn't let the great-granddaughter call him Granddad and tried her best to come between the relationships. Then she added physical abuse that steadily got more aggressive. Let's go back. He would give her access to his bank account to pay the bills as well as give her an allowance. When he retired he afforded her the same access.

HIS STORY

She smoked weed and got addicted to prescription drugs & opioids and cocaine. When her money ran out, she would get physically abusive and demand more. This cycle continued every month, and they moved a lot because she spent the household money on drugs, and he wouldn't find out until an eviction occurred. They went from having nice apartments, and owning property, in a nice neighborhood to living like they were poor. The money was still there but the poor mismanagement of money was inevitable. He would take charge of the money then after a while, give her charge and the cycle continued.

Let's back this up. His health started failing he got high blood pressure that caused kidney failure and developed diabetes.

HIS STORY

She would sneak up on him and hit him in the back of the head with a baseball bat and another time a slack on his way out the house to dialysis, or hit him on his feet with a hammer while he was leaving. Another time throw hot boiling water on his arm.

He would leave in-between each incident but again she would be so apologetic and say she wouldn't do it again, how much she loved him, and throw in his face the 40 years they been married and so forth. He would go back. They went through a vicious cycle over and over again. With him losing more of his memory because of the hits to his head, his emotional being was out of wack and his spirit was on a roller coaster ride. Things would go great leading up to pay day, but when she would have used up her allowance; she would demand more; and the cycle would continue. When she didn't get more money, the sneak attack of physical violence, would get worse: he would leave again.

HIS STORY

When he left, he would get his mind back. He started taking care of himself. He would be alright, go shopping for clothes, look for an apartment, be his old self. Then he would start listening to old love songs of the 60's and 70's and talk to her on the phone, listening to her crying and promises of doing better on top of throwing the 40 years of marriage. He would fall for it again after a couple months and go right back again.

The toxic relationship would start all over again and get more toxic each time on return. His Auntie found out that she was putting roach spray in his food and coffee.

In the last three years of 40 years, He finally left her. He went to dialysis with a mind not to return. She was poisoning him but by him going to dialysis the proof of the poison would be drained out but not the results.

HIS STORY

The doctors knew of the abuse but by now he had been beaten in the head so much he could not remember the abuse or would not admit it to the hospital staff.

Picture Deleted

because abuse was

too graphic.

He would ask his Auntie sometimes when he came to himself, "How did he get into this situation!" when did all these things happen". It was like he blacked out and didn't remember. He didn't even remember when he lost his legs or any of his hospital stays where he recovered from the abuse.

The hospital was suspicious and concerned with the injuries, symptoms and confusion but without his consent they would not act upon reporting it.

One day he went to dialysis and the hospital called his Auntie because he had a seizure and was unresponsive and rushed him to the hospital. They were not able to get in touch with the wife (she knew what she had done).
The Auntie came and sat with him the 21 days he was in a coma. There was still no contact with the wife.

He awakened finally with very little remembrance of how he got there.

HIS STORY

Let me take you back. Slowly some memory would come back but vaguely. He stayed with a relative and started going to the doctor to see about himself. He went to a podiatrist that referred him to a specialist who sent him to another specialist. To make a long story short, he had to have an amputation. Then the Pandemic hit. He went back to his cousin's house than after another doctor's appointment, he went into the hospital. His Auntie was by his side through it all and he was optimistic and eager to heal so he could get his prosthetics and learn how to walk again. Then the other leg had to be taken. He went through the operation and from the hospital went into the nursing home. Because of the pandemic no visitors were allowed in the nursing home not even family.

Prior to his release his phone was given back to him and somehow was able to get in touch with his wife and she got Power of Attorney and only one visitor allowed now. It was downhill after that.

HIS STORY

I'm telling you this story because that man, was so full of life, he would break out with a Ballard by Al Green, Jimmy Ruffin, or Jeffrey Osborn and have you mesmerized. He loved the children and would take the nephews and cousins to Wrestling or Monster Trucks Shows. He was just fun to be around. Wall to Wall Movies. He would spend time with them watching movies and playing video games or catering cooking some kind of food. You would never be hungry over his house! He did not have a mean streak in his body. He died early: because he could not **Leave and Not Look Back!**

HIS STORY

Discussions About His Story

I have not heard of any stories that the perpetrator changed through counseling or even prayer. It might be some out there, I have not heard, but compared to the abuse and number of deaths it would be a very small number if any. There were numerous 'red flags' in His Story.

He went through 40 years of abuse. They had enough money that when he retired, they could have seen the world and do whatever they wanted to do. Live where ever they wanted to live. But his whole life, very soon after adulthood was full of abuse that he got trapped in it, TRIGGERS!

Nobody talks about the men that are abused because society says that they are the stronger one. Some were raised not to hit a woman: or just have a loving heart and desire what God put man and woman together to be, or they love that hard without the understanding of what love really is. In order that your story don't end tragic, please I beg you, Get Out and Don't Look Back!

HIS STORY
Discussions About His Story

Also, the fear of the unknown can be a trigger. This is where faith has to come into being. Hope until it changes. Having to ask for help and having to tell your story can be a trigger. Recognize it and push through it. Tell somebody, talk to somebody make a plan to escape, and don't look back. Although he eventually told his story, but he hoped to much that she would change. That was false hope. Lord give us the ability to change what we can and the wisdom to know the difference. He loved her but she did not love him back and that was not going to change. Revenge and making his life miserable was all she wanted and was dead set on making that happen.

In HIS STORY he made the move to leave and left many times, but he came back, he didn't recognize the triggers and didn't take control. He came back so many times until he mentally was not able to make sound decisions because of the damage that was caused by the abuse, and that is what killed him.

TRIGGERS

Triggers-an action or situation that can lead to an adverse emotional or physical reaction.

Emotional triggers- things i.e. memories, object, a scent a song; people that spark intense negative emotions. The change in emotions can be abrupt, and in most cases, it will feel more severe than what the trigger would logically call for.

The Triggers in His Story that would make him go back was 'Love Songs', going down memory lane.

Having a warped sense of reality about his marriage and not seeing that the marriage was broken and unrepairable. What he was experiencing was not love.

Just as important as it is for a person that has given up drugs to not go in the same direction, is just as important for you to change what you listen to and what you allow yourself to look at on television; your direction, social media, or certain music genres. Sometimes we have to change the things and places that will guide our emotions into disastrous situations.

MAKE IT HAPPEN

To be successful in Making a Change. you will need:

- Courage - the ability to do something that frightens you.
- A Made-Up Mind.
- A plan – safe words, hide your ID or give to someone outside the home
- Go talk to someone totally disconnected from him/her.
- Don't be afraid to seek therapeutic support
- Seek spiritual help

Stick to your plan, what you decide on or arrange through Help lines, Safe Houses, mentors, counselors, a friend or church, it will work if you work it.

There is help waiting for you, Go!

MAKE IT HAPPEN

- Perseverance - continue in a course of action even in the face of a struggle.
- Connect to supportive services.
- Be transparent to those helping you don't be afraid to tell of your threats or risks.
- <u>Don't look Back</u> - looking back can be detrimental to your health.
- Submit to a Higher Power – trusting in God will give you a peace of mind, hope of succeeding and supernatural favor!
- Not praying false hope, Lord change him! You can pray that far-far away, but don't give into him/her changing in the moment.
- Pray Lord give me a plan and protection to get out of here and a mindset not to look back!
- Control what we let in our Ear Gates and Eye gates.
- Be willing to adapt to better possibilities.
- Change can be scary but temporary struggle can bring on awesome opportunities.

I speak in your life Strength, Courage, Peace and a determined mind to love yourself and get free!

Resources

References

Merriman-Webster Dictionary | The Holy Bible

RESOURCES

National Domestic Violence Hotline
800-799-SAFE
(800-799-7233)
Text START to 99788
www.thehotline.org

Interim House
313 259-9922
ywca@ywcadetroit.org

Turning Point, Inc Macomb County
586-463-6990
www.turningpointmacomb.org

First Step
734-722-6800
www.firststep-mi.org

D'House of Angels
16501 Wyoming
800-5937020
https://dhouseofangels.com/

Transition 123
877-463-2269

Enough Said
313-962-1920

DPD-Victim's Assistance Program
4707 St Antoine
M-167,
Detroit, MI 48201
313-833-1660

New Path
313-346-3011

Genesis House II
12900 W Chicago
313-309-5900

Lift Women's Resource Center
16280 Meyers Rd
313-345-9065

Haven
Pontiac, MI
248-334-1284
https://www.haven-oakland.org/

Freedom House Detroit
1777 N Rademacher St
Detroit, MI 48209
313-964-4320

Safe House Center
Ann Arbor, MI
27/7 Helpline:
734-995-5444

RESOURCES

Samaritas Family Center
Families with Children
30600 Michigan Ave
Westland, MI 48186
734-721-0590
https://www.samaritas.org/Bui
lding-Communities/Family-
Center

Lacasa Center
Howell, MI
24/7 Helpline
866-522-2725
517-777-8005 (Text)
https://lacasacenter.org/

International Gospel Center
375 Salliotte Rd
Ecorse, MI
313-389-2700

IGC SERVICES
336 Salliotte Road
Ecorse, MI 48229
313-383-5500

The Welcome Centre
Windsor, ON Canada
+1 519-971-7595
http://www.welcomecentreshel
ter.com/

www.ncadv.org

National Hotline

1-800-799-SAFE (7233)

Opals Project

Exiting Domestic Violence

Austin, Texas

737-225-3150

I'm giving you some resources, if you don't see your area, below is
The National Hotline:

National Domestic Violence Hotline
800-799-SAFE (800-799-7233)
Text START to 99788
www.thehotline.org

Be Blessed!

How Do You Want Your Story To End...?

Printed in the USA
CPSIA information can be obtained
at www.ICGtesting.com
LVHW090848300724
786816LV00004B/51